SUPER SKATEBOARDING™

SKATING
THE X GAMES

rosen publishing's
**rosen
central**®

New York

ALLAN B. COBB

This book is dedicated to those who strive to defy gravity

Published in 2009 by The Rosen Publishing Group, Inc.
29 East 21st Street, New York, NY 10010

Library of Congress Cataloging-in-Publication Data

Cobb, Allan B.
Skating the X Games / Allan B. Cobb.—1st ed.
    p. cm.—(Super skateboarding)
Includes bibliographical references and index.
ISBN-13: 978-1-4358-5048-4 (library binding)
ISBN-13: 978-1-4358-5392-8 (pbk)
ISBN-13: 978-1-4358-5398-0 (6 pack)
1. Skateboarding—Juvenile literature. 2. ESPN X-Games—Juvenile literature.
I. Title.
GV859.8.C63 2009
796.04'6—dc22

2008017738

Manufactured in the United States of America

On the cover: An X Games skater pulls a McTwist on the vert ramp.

CONTENTS

INTRODUCTION

Shaun White flies during the men's vert skateboard finals in the 2006 X Games.

Skateboarding was born in the 1950s, when California surfers put roller skate wheels on wooden boxes. No one is sure who invented the skateboard because it seems that several people came up with the idea at about the same time. Soon, the wooden boxes were replaced with wood planks and the roller skate wheels were replaced with trucks, and the modern skateboard was born.

Most of the early skateboarders were surfers. Skateboarding was seen as a way to surf on dry land. These surfers mostly did either downhill slalom or freestyle skateboarding. Torger Johnson, Woody Woodward, and Danny Berer were some of the early skateboarding pioneers. By the mid-1960s, the skateboarding fad had lost its popularity and had almost died out. Skateboarding came and went over the years until its popularity rose again in the 1990s. As more people began skateboarding, competition was born.

The sports network ESPN started organizing a national competition of extreme sports and decided to add skateboarding to the lineup. This helped propel skateboarding into the sport it is today and helped launch the X Games.

The X Games are an annual event with a focus on extreme action sports. The X Games are now divided into two parts: the Winter X Games, held in January or February, and the Summer X Games, held in August. Skateboarding is held in August as part of the Summer X Games. Competitors perform as best as they can to win gold, silver, or bronze medals and prize money. The X Games hold international competitions and demos around the world at varying times throughout the year. In recent years, the X Games have been shown live on ESPN and ABC television.

CHAPTER ONE

THE X GAMES EXPLAINED

The skateboarding competition currently features six disciplines. They are street/park men's, street/park women's, vert men's, vert women's, men's best trick, and big air. The street/park competition showcases skaters performing tricks in a concrete plaza, complete with stair sets, banks, manual pads, and ledges. Vert features competitors on a 120-foot-wide (36.6-meter-wide) ramp, complete with 11-foot (3.6 m) transitions and 2 feet (.6 m) of vert. Best trick skaters flow wall to wall and combine big air and technical lip tricks. Big air skaters take jumps that are scored on style, creativity, and amplitude. Each discipline has its own competition format, competition flow, and scoring.

The vert, vert doubles, and street/park competitions are judged by a team of six judges. One judge is designated as the head judge. Each judge scores each competitor on a whole-number point scale with one hundred being a perfect score. Competitions are divided into heats, sessions, and/or finals depending on the event. How each competition is run will be discussed below. After each grouping of runs, the head judge collects all the scores. The highest score and the lowest score for each competitor are thrown out, and the four remaining scores are added together and divided by four. This gives each competitor a score that is recorded to two decimal places. The competitors are then ranked on the leaderboard based on their score. The competitor with the highest score is in first place and wins a gold medal. The competitor in second place wins a silver medal, and third place wins a bronze medal.

Vert

The vert men's starts with twenty competitors divided into two groups of ten. Competitors in each group take two forty-five-second runs, and they are scored by the judges. Competitors are scored on aggressiveness and difficulty of maneuvers, variety of maneuvers and lines in the run, use of the ramp, amplitude, originality, and style on a 13-foot (4-m) half-pipe. Once their scores are established, the top ten competitors move forward to the vert finals.

Andy Macdonald demonstrates why he is a solid competitor in the 2006 X Games men's vert finals.

In the finals, the top ten competitors each take three forty-five-second runs, and they are scored again on the same criteria. The head judge collects the scores, discards the highest and lowest, and finds the average. The competitor's highest score on any run is kept and becomes the competitor's final score. The competitors are listed on the leaderboard according to their final score.

The vert women's competition is run in a different format and has different scoring than the vert men's. The vert women's contest starts with eight competitors. Each competitor is randomly assigned to a start

Street Versus Vert

The world of skateboarding has two big rivalries: street and vert. Street skating is done on any surface or structure commonly found in an urban area. It may be a parking lot, handrail on stairs, a bench, or a curb. Street skating first came about in the 1970s as soon as skateboard tricks started. Street skaters considered themselves to be the rebels of the sport because they performed radical tricks on everyday objects.

Vert skating is done with a vertical ramp built specifically for skateboarding. It started when skaters used the curved surfaces of empty swimming pools. Soon, skaters figured out that they could build ramps, quarter-pipes, and half-pipes to have better control. Today, vert skating has evolved into more of an art form with skaters performing very specialized tricks.

Street skaters still consider themselves to be the rebels of skating. They learn their tricks—often without any safety gear—in out-of-the-way places around town. The better skaters can become professionals and compete in competitions. These skaters can get contracts from sponsors such as apparel and accessory companies and may make up to ten thousand dollars a month.

order. The competition is a thirty-minute jam session. After each competitor takes a run in the start order, she may take as many random runs as she wishes until the allotted time for the jam ends.

Judges do not assign a number score to each run. Instead, the judges make notes on how well each competitor did on a run. The notes record the judge's overall impression of originality, difficulty, style, height, distance, and execution. The judges compare notes and place the competitors in order based on the results. The competitors are then ranked on the leaderboard.

Street/Park

The selection session for street starts with nineteen skateboarders. They compete to reach the Elite 9 for the finals. The first-place skater

Andrew Reynolds performs a high ollie off the quarter-pipe in the X Games street finals.

from previous year's competition is automatically qualified for the finals. This brings the total number of competitors to ten in the finals.

The selection session has three sessions lasting approximately thirty minutes each. Competitors are divided into three heats. Competitors are randomly assigned to a heat. Two of the heats have six competitors, and the other has seven competitors. The head judge selects the obstacles that the heats will skate in the session. Street skaters compete in a true street competition with a variety of obstacles. Skaters will grind, ollie onto or over concrete ledges and benches, jump stairs and gaps, and boardslide down handrails.

Each heat lasts seven minutes, and the competitors in the heat will skate the chosen obstacles. Each judge assigns each competitor in each heat a score based on the tricks performed by the competitor and the judge's impressions of how well the competitor performed.

At the end of each selection session, the judge's scores are recorded for each competitor. The highest and lowest scores for each competitor are thrown out, and an average score of the remaining four serves as the competitor's score for that session. After all three sessions, the competitor's three session scores are averaged for the session score. The top nine competitors advance to the finals to meet the winner from the previous year.

The finals consist of three sessions lasting fifteen minutes each. The competitors are not broken down into heats. The head judge selects the course and obstacles for the finals. All ten competitors skate for the entire session. After each session, each competitor's highest and lowest scores are thrown out and an average score is assigned. After all three sessions, the average of each competitor's three session scores is used to determine the final score. Competitors are listed on the leaderboard in the order of their final score.

Unlike the street/park men's, the women's competition begins with eight women and only has a finals session. The finals session is three seven-minute sessions where all competitors skate together. The head judge selects the section and obstacles on the course to be used for sessions. Obstacles may include concrete ledges, benches, stairs, gaps, and handrails. As the competitors skate, the judges record scores for all the competitors based on the tricks performed and the judge's impression of how well the competitor performs.

After each session, each judge reviews his or her notes and individually assigns competitors a whole-number score. After throwing out the highest score and the lowest score, an average is taken for the remaining scores. After all three sessions, the competitor's score for each session is added together and an average is taken. This serves as the competitor's final score. The competitors are listed on the leaderboard based on their final scores.

Vert Doubles

The vert doubles consists of ten teams of two competitors. The teams are divided into two groups. Each team of competitors in each group completes two thirty- to forty-five-second runs. Teams are judged on originality, difficulty, flow, use of ramp, combination tricks, interaction of the partners, and amplitude. The judges score each team. As in other competitions, the highest and lowest scores are thrown out and an average of the remaining scores is taken. The top five teams from both groups advance to the finals.

In the finals, each of the five teams completes two thirty- to forty-five-second runs starting with the team having the lowest score, with the highest-scoring team going last. Again, the judges score the teams.

After all the teams have completed their runs, the judge's scores are gathered and the highest and lowest for each team are thrown out. An average is taken of the remaining scores, and the results are posted on the leaderboard.

Best Trick

The best trick competition is scored by judges who give points based on originality, difficulty, style, height, and execution. This takes place as a forty-five-minute jam session. Skaters take turns performing tricks during the entire period of the jam. Unique and creative tricks are just as important in scoring as is the difficulty of the tricks. This competition often brings out the cutting-edge skateboarding tricks. After the session is over, the judges get together and go over their notes. They assign the skaters a ranking based on their notes, and the results are posted on the leaderboard.

Big Air

The big air competitors skate down a 60- to 80-foot-high (18.3- to 24.4-m) roll-in, launch over a gap 50 or 70 feet (15.2 or 21.3 m), and continue into a 27-foot (8.2-m) quarter-pipe. The selection session is made up of nine competitors who each make four runs on the big air. Each run is scored by five judges. Scoring by the judges is based on style, creativity, and amplitude. After all competitors have completed their four runs, the judges meet and determine the scores. The highest and lowest scores for each competitor's run are thrown out. The three remaining scores are added together and averaged. The average scores for each of the competitor's four runs are added together and averaged. The results are

Andy Macdonald catches air in the 2005 big air competition.

posted on the leaderboard, and the top three competitors from the selection session advance to the finals.

In the finals, the three leaders from the selection session meet up with the previous year's top three finalists. The six competitors each make five runs on the big air. Each run is scored. After all the competitors have taken their five runs, the judges meet and the scoring is done like in the selection session. The scores are then posted on the leaderboard in the order of their ranking.

Equipment

The skateboards used by all competitors are usually made from seven-ply maple laminate. The trucks are attached to the deck, and competitors are allowed to select their wheels. The wheels are made of urethane and vary in hardness based on the type of skating and the preference of the competitor.

All competitors must wear a helmet during competition. Competitors may choose to wear other protective gear, such as gloves, elbow pads, and knee pads. Most competitors choose to wear knee pads and elbow pads, and many choose to wear gloves. The risk of falling during competition is high, and the safety equipment helps prevent injuries. Most competitors wear shorts and T-shirts from their sponsors.

Pumping

1. Enter the curved part of the ramp (the transition) while bending or compressing your knees.
2. As you hit the flat bottom of the half-pipe, you straighten or uncompress your knees.
3. This lowers your center of gravity while you are on the curved surface, allowing you to gain speed.
4. As you reach the lip, stand straight up.
5. As you ride back down, compress your knees once again to gain speed.
6. Regain your balance and prepare for your next trick.

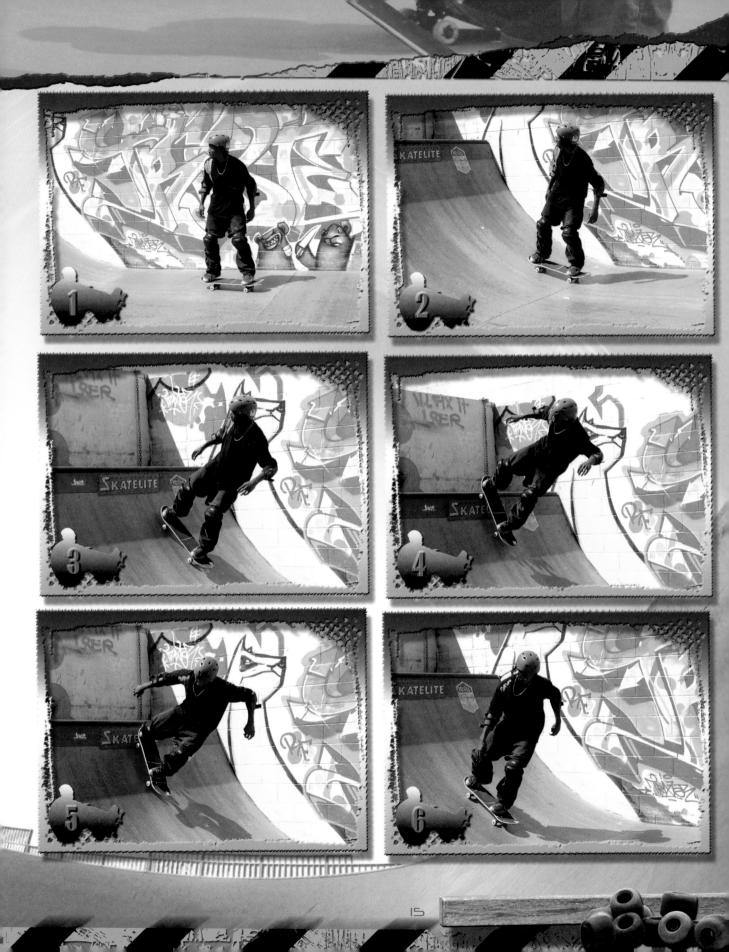

CHAPTER TWO

HOW IT ALL STARTED

The 1990s saw an explosion of awareness in extreme sports. Young people were jumping, skating, and riding in new and exciting ways. Skateboarding and other extreme sports, such as bungee jumping, BMX, and street luge, also became popular and very competitive. However, many conventional sports fans saw these people as daredevils rather than athletes. Even though most overlooked their accomplishments, they continued to push the boundaries of their sports.

Creating the Extreme Concept

ESPN, the cable television sports network, saw an opportunity to showcase the young talents of these extreme sports. The ESPN management decided to create an international gathering of alternative sports athletes. In 1993, Ron Semiao, the father of the X Games, assembled a team to develop the concept. It took two years to develop the concept and create a competition they called the Extreme Games.

ESPN promoted the Extreme Games and chose Rhode Island as the site. In June 1995, the Extreme Games started. Venues for the Extreme Games were held in Newport, Providence, and Middletown, Rhode Island, and Mount Snow, Vermont. Young athletes competed in

The Extreme Games concept was built around extreme sports, in which young athletes use nontraditional sports to show off their talents.

Tony Hawk

Tony Hawk was born on May 12, 1968, in San Diego, California. He is considered one of the "old men" of vert skating. Hawk is credited with the invention of more than eighty vert tricks, including the stalefish, Madonna, and McHawk. He is famous for being the first recorded skater to land the 900 (two-and-a-half rotations in the air before landing back on the ramp) during a televised competition.

Hawk has been very successful in starting and running several skateboard-related businesses. When he is not competing in competitions or running his business, he volunteers with youth groups and acts as a skateboard ambassador. Hawk is probably one of the most recognized skateboarders. He has been the subject of many articles and books, has written an autobiography, has appeared on television and in movies, and has won many awards.

twenty-seven events in nine sport categories: bungee jumping, eco-challenge, in-line skating, skateboarding, skysurfing, sport climbing, street luge, biking, and water sports. The skateboarding competition had two categories: men's vert and men's street. The street luge is an event where the racers pilot highly modified skateboards downhill at high speeds.

Almost two hundred thousand fans attended the Extreme Games, and they were carried live on ESPN. Seven sponsors provided money and prizes for the Extreme Games. The sponsors were Advil, Mountain Dew, Taco Bell, Chevy Trucks, AT&T, Nike, and Miller Lite Ice. The men's vert was won by Tony Hawk, and the men's street was won by Chris Senn.

The Extreme Games were considered a success by the athletes, organizers, spectators, producers, and sponsors. The overwhelming popularity of the Extreme Games 1995 made it easy for ESPN to decide to hold the event the following year. Rhode Island was again chosen to be the venue for the games.

1996: The First "X Games"

In January 1996, the event's name was officially changed to the X Games. The name change came about for many reasons. The name "X Games" is much easier to translate into other languages and thus expands the appeal of the games internationally. Of course, the catchier name also provided better branding opportunities for merchandise. That June, another two hundred thousand spectators came out for the X Games.

Chris Senn soars to a silver medal in the 1996 X Games in the street finals.

Skateboarding again proved popular, and the competition included men's vert and men's street. Andy Macdonald took the men's vert by beating out Tony Hawk, and Rodil de Araujo Jr. took the men's street, beating out Chris Senn.

Andy Macdonald is considered one of the best vert skaters in the world. He missed the 2007 X Games due to a knee injury, but he is expected to continue competing. He was born on July 31, 1973, and started skating in 1986. He started competing in 1994 and turned pro in 1996. He is still one of the top vert skaters today. He has won many gold medals in the X Games, and he won the World Cup of Skateboarding eight times. Macdonald is still a strong skater, and he continues to compete.

The success of the 1996 X Games established that the competition was strong enough to continue into the future. To expand the appeal of the event, the decision was made to move the X Games to California.

Frontside Kick Turn

1. First, position your feet with one foot forward directly above the bolts of the front truck.
2. Your rear foot should be just behind the rear truck.
3. Your knees should be slightly bent.
4. Then, while moving at a comfortable speed, use your front foot to flick the board to get it moving.
5. Control the board with your front foot and make it pivot around on the rear wheels.
6. Ride back down the transition.

CHAPTER THREE

THE EARLY YEARS

San Diego and Oceanside, California, were chosen as the venues for the X Games III from June 20 through June 28, 1997. On the West Coast, the X Games attracted more than 220,000 fans. Changes were made to the competitions, but skateboarding remained a popular event. In fact, it was so popular that a new skateboarding event was added—men's vert doubles. In this event, two-man teams compete for points in the vert arena. The overwhelming success of the X Games in California led to an invitation to have them again in 1998 at the same location.

Once again, Tony Hawk performed magnificently to win the men's vert. Chris Senn repeated his 1995 strong performance and won the men's street. A team of Tony Hawk and Andy Macdonald took the first men's vert double.

Chris Senn has been one of the top competitive skaters since the middle of the 1990s, and his success continues even today. He was born on December 12, 1972, in Grass Valley, California. He started skating in 1983.

In 1995, Senn was voted *Thrasher* magazine Skater of the Year. He has won three gold medals in the X Games. He is a strong competitor in the street/park events. His spontaneous and aggressive style makes him exciting to watch in competition. He continues to skate professionally to this very day.

Skateboarding legend Tony Hawk performs a trick on a half-pipe in the 1998 X Games.

Tony Hawk's 900

The 900 is a 2.5-revolution (900°) spin that is considered to be one of skateboarding's rarest tricks because of the difficulty and technical skill required to perform it. Tony Hawk was the first to successfully perform the trick on film in the 1999 X Games after ten failed attempts. His success came after the allotted time, but because of the nature of the trick, the judges allowed it to stand and none of the other competitors protested.

Hawk managed to pull off another 900 in the 2001 X Games, but it, too, was after the allotted time. In the 2003 X Games, Hawk succeeded in pulling off the 900 with seven seconds left in regulation time. The only other competitors who have managed this trick are Giorgio Zattoni, Sandro Dias, and Shaun White.

1998: X Games IV

The format of the X Games saw more changes in 1998. In April, the first international X Games qualifying event was held in Phuket Island, Thailand. The Asian X Games qualifier featured two hundred athletes from the Pacific Rim competing for a limited number of spots in the San Diego X Games.

In June, the X Games set a new attendance record for the fourth straight year. More than 233,000 fans descended on Mariner's Point in San Diego, California, for the fourth annual X Games. The ever-popular skateboarding venue again included men's vert, men's street/park, and men's vert doubles.

In the men's vert, Andy Macdonald bested Tony Hawk for the top prize. In the vert doubles, Tony Hawk and Andy Macdonald proved untouchable and took the top prize. In the men's street, Rodil de Araujo Jr. came out on top of the competition.

Rodil de Araujo Jr. is a strong force in skating. He was born April 12, 1979, in Curitiba, Brazil. He began skating in 1989 and turned pro in 1991. He has been a successful competitor for many years. In 2002, he won three gold medals at the X Games. He has always made good showings and is a strong competitor. Overall, he has won ten gold and silver medals in the X Games.

The half-pipe is one of the arenas where skateboarders show off their best tricks.

1999: X Games V

From June 27 to July 4, the San Francisco X Games attracted nearly 275,000 fans. Skateboarding again received more and more attention from the fans. One of the most memorable events of the 1999 X Games was Tony Hawk's first skateboarding 900 to win the Best Vert Trick.

Again, the skateboarding events included men's vert, men's street/park, men's vert doubles. This year, the men's vert was due for a change. Bucky Lasek beat out Hawk (92.00) and Andy Macdonald (93.00) to take the top honors, with a 94.25. In the men's double vert, Hawk and Macdonald showed that they still had what it took to take the top honors, with a 95.25. The men's street top honors went once again to Chris Senn, who scored 91.75.

Lasek is regarded as one of the most innovative vert skateboarders. He shows off his talent by mastering technical tricks that most skaters avoid. One of his specialties is being able to pull off an entire vert run switch, or riding opposite of his natural stance. Lasek is a powerful force in vert competitions. He is also highly aggressive and strongly motivated to conquer new skateboarding territory, though he sticks to vert. He has won six gold medals in the X Games.

2000: X Games VI

The 2000 X Games hosted more than 350 of the world's best alternative sports athletes in San Francisco, California. Between August 17 and 22, they competed for nearly one million dollars in prize money and medals.

The ever-popular skateboarding venue was also expanded. New in 2000 was the men's best trick vert. In this competition, competitors gave their best trick performance to try and win the gold. The lineup

Andy Macdonald (left) bounces off of Tony Hawk's skateboard as part of a gold medal performance in the 2000 X Games.

of events in 2000 included men's vert, men's street, men's vert doubles, and men's best trick vert.

Bucky Lasek again took the gold in the men's vert, scoring a 98.50 and beating Pierre-Luc Gagnon's 95.00. The unstoppable team of Tony Hawk and Andy Macdonald took the gold in the men's vert doubles for the fourth time, with a 93.50. In an upset, Eric Koston took the gold in the men's street, with a 93.50. The first year of the men's best trick vert, Bob Burnquist took the gold with his execution of a fakie 5-0 and fakie kickflip out off of the grind bar.

Bob Burnquist scores a 98.00 with his execution of tricks to win the men's vert competition in 2001.

2001: X Games VII

In 2001, the X Games moved to First Union Complex, Philadelphia, Pennsylvania, and was held August 17 to 22. Skateboarding continued to draw large crowds. The skateboard events included men's vert, men's vert doubles, men's street, and men's best trick vert.

Bob Burnquist won the gold in the men's vert contest with an unbelievable 98, the highest point average ever given to any athlete in skateboarding. His line McTwists, kickflips, switch indy kickflips, fakie 540s, and switch kickflips made him unstoppable. The team of Tony Hawk and Andy Macdonald continued to dominate the men's double vert with two nearly flawless runs. They only managed to practice together for two days two weeks prior to the X Games. Kerry Getz took gold in the men's street, hitting all the obstacles with style. His 92.60 was more than enough to beat out Eric Koston's 86.30. Matt Dove had a controversial win for gold in the men's best trick vert when he landed a varial 720 on his tenth try. He landed the trick after time had run out, but the decision was to credit him with it.

2002: X Games VIII

The 2002 X Games took place at First Union Complex in Philadelphia, Pennsylvania, from August 15 to 19. More than 220,000 fans came out to the games, and nearly sixty-three million people tuned in on television. The popularity of skateboarding required the addition of another park course. Women's skateboard exhibitions were featured between the men's competitions.

The skateboard competitions included men's vert, men's vert doubles, men's street, men's park, men's best trick vert, and men's best trick street. The expanded venue with the additional skate park course allowed the addition of the men's street and the men's park events.

Pierre-Luc Gagnon managed to take the gold in the men's vert through consistent skating that scored him a 96.75. His competitors—Burnquist, MacDonald, Jake Brown, and Lasek—just could not pull off enough tricks to beat him. Gagnon beat the second-place Burnquist by more than six points. The seemingly unbeatable team of Tony Hawk and Andy Macdonald again took the gold in the men's double vert for the sixth straight year, with a 95.50. Rodil de Araujo Jr. stopped all the competition and took the gold in both the men's street and the men's park events. Pierre-Luc Gagnon took home his second gold in 2002 by winning the men's best trick vert with a heel flip McTwist. Rodil de Araujo Jr. took home his third gold for 2002 by winning the best trick street event.

Boardside

1. Start by getting up to speed and approaching the lip or rail at a slight angle.
2. The front of your body should be facing away from the lip.
3. As you approach the lip, pop a 90-degree ollie that is just high enough for your front truck to clear the lip.
4. You want to make contact with the board as parallel to the lip as possible. If you land a bit off, you can usually correct by shifting your weight to one side or the other.
5. When you have your balance, lean forward slightly and use your arms to maintain your balance.
6. To finish, lift your front trucks off the lip and finish your roll.

CHAPTER FOUR

THE X GAMES TODAY

In 2003, the X Games returned to California but moved to Los Angeles. The games were held August 14 to 17. The main venue was the Staples Center. Additional venues were around Los Angeles, including the Los Angeles Coliseum. The attendance for the event was more than 180,000 fans. The X Games were carried on ESPN, ESPN2, and ABC Sports.

Skateboarding continued to be popular. That year, a category was added for women: the women's park. Men competed in men's vert, men's vert doubles, men's street, men's park, men's best trick vert, and men's best trick street.

As usual, the competition was strong for the events. Bucky Lasek returned to take the gold in the men's vert. The team of Lasek and Bob Burnquist put on the best show and finally took the gold in the men's vert doubles with the highest score ever given. Eric Koston took the gold in the men's street after arriving only ten minutes before the competition began. Ryan Sheckler took the gold for men's park. Tony Hawk was back in style to take the gold in men's best trick vert with the first-ever 900 within competition time. Hawk announced his retirement from competition after the X Games.

Chad Muska skated to the gold in the men's best trick vert, which surprised everyone, as he had not competed in years. Vanessa Torres was

Bucky Lasek poses for the cameras after being awarded a gold medal for the 2003 vert competition.

Big air pioneer Danny Way drops into the ramps during a practice run in the 2004 X Games.

the first woman to win the gold in the skateboarding competition in the women's park event.

2004: X Games X

The tenth anniversary of the X Games was held again in Los Angeles from August 5 to 8. As a new feature, a finals-only format was broadcast live. Attendance over the four-day period totaled 170,471 fans. The action was carried live on ESPN, ESPN2, and ABC Sports. While attendance was low, the finals-only format was a big success on television.

Skateboarding continued to gain viewers and become even more popular. This year, the women's park event was replaced with the women's vert and the women's street events. The men's park was dropped. Another new event was added, and it quickly became very popular. The big air event was added with its huge ramp, jump, and quarter-pipe. The men competed in men's vert, men's street, men's best trick vert, and big air.

The competition was strong among the skaters. Bucky Lasek again took the gold for men's vert. Paul Rodriguez made a strong showing and took the gold in the men's street event. Sandro Dias made a strong performance and took the gold in the best trick vert category, where he pulled a 900 over the channel. The big air competition was soundly taken by Danny Way with an incredible performance. The women's vert gold was awarded to Lyn-Z Adams Hawkins for her strong performance. Elissa Steamer proved unbeatable and took the gold in the women's street event by being the only woman to kickflip down the nine-stair set.

2005: X Games XI

In 2005, the X Games were held in Los Angeles from August 4 to 7. The venues for the games were the Home Depot Center, Staples Center, Long Beach Marine Stadium, and surfing's new home of Puerto Escondido,

The Mega Ramp

The Mega Ramp stands 62 feet (18.9 m) tall and 293 feet (89.3 m) long. When it was first introduced to the X Games in 2003, it was set up outside. In 2007, the Mega Ramp as moved inside the Staples Center. This move made the Mega Ramp seem even larger.

A ride on the Mega Ramp begins by taking an elevator to the top-floor landing. Skaters choose either a 60- or 80-foot (18.3 m or 24.4 m) roll-in to a ramp. After leaving the ramp, they jump either a 50- or 70-foot (15.2 m or 21.3 m) gap. After landing, skaters ride up a 27-foot-tall (8.2 m) quarter-pipe that propels them as high as 50 feet (15.2 m). Runs are judged on difficulty and execution of tricks done over both jumps.

Mexico. The event was broadcast live in more than seventy-five countries. This international coverage expanded viewership and increased international awareness of the games.

The lineup in skateboarding events remained the same as in 2004. Competitors from the United States and around the world competed in men's vert, men's street, men's best trick vert, women's vert, women's street, and big air. The competition was strong, and audiences were left satisfied.

Bob Burnquist performs a blunt to fakie on the table to help him take the gold medal in the men's vert best trick competition in the 2005 X Games.

Pierre-Luc Gagnon came back to take the gold in the men's vert by breaking a tie with Shaun White on his final run by landing a switch heel flip 360 repeat for a score of 95.00. Paul Rodriguez returned to take the gold in the men's street event, scoring a 92.50. Bob Burnquist took the gold in best trick vert with a frontside 540 Nar-Jar and a blunt to fakie, beating out Shaun White, who could not land a 1080. The women's vert gold went to Cara-Beth Burnside for her consistent skating. The women's street again went to Elissa Steamer, the oldest of the female competitors. Danny Way dominated the big air event to take home the gold again, even though he had a broken foot from his jump over the Great Wall of China.

Way is the king of the Mega Ramp. He was born April 15, 1974, in Portland, Oregon. Way started skating in 1981, entered his first competition in 1986, and turned pro in 1988. As a vert skater, he is the best at getting big air. In late 2002, Way built the first Mega Ramp. With it, he set a new ramp-to-ramp record of 65 feet (19.8 m) and a new highest air record of 18 feet, 3 inches (5.6 m). He built a second version of the Mega Ramp, and on June 19, 2003, he broke two world records in one run: the longest ramp-to-ramp record at 75 feet (22.9 m), and the highest air at 23.5 feet (7.2 m).

2006: X Games XII

Los Angeles again hosted the X Games from August 3 to 6 at the Home Depot Center and the Staples Center. The attendance was down to about 140,000 fans, but television viewership increased nearly 13 percent over the 2005 X Games. For the first time, coverage of the X Games was aired twenty-four hours each day of the event using ESPN, ESPN2, ABC, ESPN Classic, EXPN.com, ESPN360, Mobile ESPN, ESPN International, and iTunes.

The popularity of skateboarding was as strong as ever. The events included men's vert, men's street/park, men's best trick vert, women's vert, women's street, and big air. These offerings thrilled fans and attracted many new viewers as the competition among the skaters increased.

Sandro Dias jumped ahead to take the gold in the men's vert. Chris Cole skated to the gold in the men's street category after putting together a run consisting almost entirely of no-complys and airwalks. Bucky Lasek took the gold in the men's vert event. Cara-Beth Burnside showed again that she was a strong skater to take the gold in the women's vert. Elissa Steamer continued her domination of the women's street competition.

Sandro Dias soars during the 2006 men's vert finals. His performance won him the gold in this event.

Danny Way showed his skills in the big air event to easily take the gold, scoring a 95.00 and landing the first and second ever backflip off the ramp.

Cara-Beth "CB" Burnside is the first woman to dominate the women's competitions in the X Games. She was born on July 23, 1968, in Orange, California. Burnside started skating in 1978, and she began competing in 1994 against men. She is considered one of the first extreme female athletes. She excels not only in skateboarding but also in snowboarding. She has won two gold medals in the X Games for skateboarding. As a snowboarder, she has competed in the X Games and in the Winter Olympics.

Elissa Steamer is another strong female skater. Steamer was born on July 31, 1975, in Fort Myers, Florida. She began skating in 1989 and turned pro in 1998. She is considered one of the best female street skaters, and she has three X Games gold medals to back that up. She has been winning competitions both in the United States and internationally since turning pro.

2007: X Games XIII

In 2007, the X Games returned to Los Angeles from August 2 to 5. The venues included the Home Depot Center and the Staples Center. Attendance remained about the same as in 2006, but television and online viewership increased as even more attention was given to the games.

Skateboarding continued to grow in popularity. Viewership and recognition of skateboarding continued to grow as athletes fiercely competed for the gold. The events for 2007 were men's vert, men's street, men's best trick street, men's vert amateurs, women's vert, women's street, and big air.

As usual, all the skaters gave strong performances. The gold for men's vert went to Shaun White, who beat out veterans like Gagnon,

MacDonald, and Lasek. Chris Cole skated ahead to take the gold in the men's street event, with a 94.33, barely beating Greg Lutzka's 93.41. Chris Cole also took the gold in the men's best trick street event after landing a 360 double flip. Ben Hatchell took the gold in the men's vert amateurs. Lyn-Z Adams Hawkins took the gold in the women's vert by beating out seasoned pros Cara-Beth Burnside and Mimi Knoop. Marisa Dal Santo skated to gold in the women's street by beating out Elissa Steamer. Bob Burnquist won the gold on his final run when he pulled a switch-stance backside ollie over the 70-foot (21.3-m) gap. On the quarter-pipe, he landed a switch-stance frontside 540. Burnquist was in second place behind Jake Brown until he took a fall.

The X Games had a near tragedy when competitor Jake Brown failed a big air stunt resulting in a fall. He fell from more than 40 feet (12.2 m) in the air and landed on his backside and back. After eight minutes of lying motionless while being checked out by medics, he walked away with help. He suffered a fractured wrist, a bruised lung and liver, whiplash, a ruptured spleen, and a concussion.

The success of the X Games and skateboarding has ensured that the X Games will continue. The X Games are scheduled to continue in Los Angeles until at least 2010.

Tail Slide

1. To start this trick, start in the ollie position with your back foot slight closer to the heel side of your skateboard. Ride parallel up the ramp's edge.
2. Do an ollie.
3. Land with the tail of the skateboard on the obstacle.
4. You must keep pressure on your back foot.
5. This keeps your board from sliding off.
6. To get off the obstacle, push the board off the obstacle.

GLOSSARY

airs Tricks that involve floating in the air while using a hand to hold the board on the feet or by keeping constant and careful pressure on the board with the feet to keep it from floating away.

amplitude Height of airs or length of grinds by a competitor in the vert competitions.

big air An X Game event that uses the Mega Ramp to propel skaters more than 50 feet (15.2 m) into the air.

grinds Tricks where the skateboarder slides on the hangers of the trucks. Grinds are performed on any object that may fit between the space between the wheels where the trucks meet.

leaderboard A display that shows the leaders and rankings in a competition.

900 The 900 is a 2.5-revolution (900°) spin that is considered to be one of skateboarding's most difficult tricks.

quarter-pipe A ramp that resembles a quarter of the cross section of a pipe.

ramp An incline used to attain "air" by skateboarders.

roll-in The ramp used to gain speed at the start of the Mega Ramp.

street Street skating is done on any surface or structure found in an urban area. It may be a parking lot, the handrail on stairs, a bench, or a curb.

vert Vert skating is done with a vertical ramp built especially for skateboarding.

FOR MORE INFORMATION

Birdhouse Skateboards
15272 Jason Circle
Huntington Beach, CA 92649
(714) 379-0020
Web site: http://www.birdhouseskateboards.com
Birdhouse is a manufacturer of custom skateboard decks, complete skateboards,
    wheels, and accessories.

Powell Peralta
Skate One Corporation
30 S. La Patera Lane
(800) 288-7528
Web site: http://www.powell-peralta.com
Santa Barbara, CA 93117
Powell Peralta is a manufacturer of skateboard decks.

SBC Skateboard Magazine
2255 B Queen Street East, Suite 3266
Toronto, ON M4E-1G3
Canada
(416) 406-2400
Web site: http://www.sbcskateboard.com
This magazine is a source of skateboarding news and information from around Canada.

Skaters for Public Skateparks (SPS)
820 N. River Street, Loft 206
Portland, OR 97227

(540) 219-4096

Web site: http://http://www.skatepark.org

SPS is a nonprofit skate park advocacy organization, international in reach, dedicated
to providing the information necessary to ensure that safe, rewarding, freely
accessible skate parks are available to all skateboarders.

Skull Skates
PD's Hot Shop
2868 West 4th Avenue
Vancouver, BC V6K1R2
Canada
(604) 739.7796
Web site: http://www.skullskates.com

Skull Skates is a manufacturer of skateboards and skate products in Canada.

Web Site

Due to the changing nature of Internet links, Rosen Publishing has
developed an online list of Web sites related to the subject of this book.
This site is updated regularly. Please use this link to access the list:

http://www.rosenlinks.com/ssk/sxg

FOR FURTHER READING

Crossingham, John. *Extreme Skateboarding*. New York, NY: Crabtree Publishing Company, 2004.

Dieterich, Alice. *Tony Hawk, Andy Macdonald: Ride to the Top*. New York, NY: Grosset & Dunlap, 2003.

Gutman, Dan. *Getting Air*. New York, NY: Simon & Schuster Books for Young Readers, 2007.

Hocking, Justin. *Rippin' Ramps: A Skateboarder's Guide to Riding Half-Pipes*. New York, NY: Rosen Publishing Group, 2005.

Miller, Connie Colwell. *Skateboarding Big Air*. Mankato, MN: Capstone Press, 2007.

Rosenberg, Aaron. *Advanced Skateboarding: From Kick Turns to Catching Air*. New York, NY: Rosen Publishing Group, 2003.

Rosenberg, Aaron. *A Beginner's Guide to Very Cool Skateboarding Tricks*. New York, NY: Rosen Publishing Group, 2003.

Savage, Jeff. *The X Games: Skateboarding's Greatest*. Mankato, MN: Capstone Press, 2006.

Spencer, Russ. *Skateboarding*. Mankato, MN: Child's World, 2005.

BIBLIOGRAPHY

Buck, Ron. "Hawk Soars into History with 900." 1999. Retrieved March 18, 2008 (http://espn.go.com/xgames/summerx99/skate/news/1999/990628/01329413.html).

Crossland, George. "X Games Vert and Big Air." 2006. Retrieved March 19, 2008 (http://www.skateboardermag.com/skateboarder-news-features/features/xgmsvrtbgair/index.html).

Dodd, Daniel. "Senn Takes His Skating in Stride." 1999. Retrieved March 18, 2008 (http://espn.go.com/xgames/summerx99/skate/news/1999/990627/01328339.html).

Donaldson, Keith Eric. "Attack of the Killer B's." 2003. Retrieved March 18, 2008 (http://expn.go.com/expn/story?id=2920886).

Fenton, Mary. " W Skate Street: Elissa Steam-Rolls." 2006. Retrieved March 18, 2008 (http://expn.go.com/expn/story?pageName=050805_w_skatestreet).

Krolick, Joe. "Andre Genovesi 'wait for something dope.'" 2008. Retrieved March 19, 2008 (http://www.thrashermagazine.com/index.php?option=com_content&task=view&id=592&Itemid=68).

Skateboarder Magazine. "How Much Do Pro Skateboarders Make?" Retrieved March 19, 2008 (http://www.skateboardermag.com/skateboarder-news-features/news/howmuch/index.html).

Transworld Skateboarding. "Jake Brown – Best Vert Award." 2005. Retrieved March 19, 2008 (http://www.skateboarding.com/article.jsp?ID=1000008288&typeID=419).

Zitzer, Paul. "15 Things You Didn't Know About Tony Hawk." 2003. Retrieved March 19, 2008 (http://skateboardermag.com/skateboarder-news-features/features/15tonyhawk/index.html).

INDEX

X

About the Author

Allan B. Cobb is an author who writes on a wide variety of topics. He has published more than twenty books for young adults. When not writing, he enjoys many extreme pursuits. He fills his free time by caving, sailing, kayaking, backpacking, rock climbing, snorkeling, scuba diving, and hiking. He travels often throughout the United States, Mexico, and Central America.

Photo Credits

Cover (right), pp. 1, 34 Harry How/Getty Images; cover (left) www.istockphoto.com/ Sergey Baykov; cover (background) Tom Hauck/Allsport/Getty Images; p. 3 © www. istockphoto.com / Shane White; pp. 4-5 (skateboard and background) © www.istock-photo.com / Richardson Maneze; pp. 4 (inset), 7, 38 Jeff Gross/Getty Images; pp. 9, 19 © AP Images; p. 13 Nick Laham/Getty Images; pp. 15, 21, 31, 41 © Tony Donaldson/ Icon SMI/The Rosen Publishing Group; p. 17 Mike Powell/ Getty Images; p. 23 Tom Hauck/Getty Images; p. 25 Lutz Bongarts/Bongarts/Getty Images; p. 27 David Leeds/ Getty Images; p. 28 Ezra Shaw/Allsport/Getty Images; p. 33 Chris Polk/WireImage; p. 36 Mike Ehrmann/WireImage; cover and interior background and decorative elements © www.istockphoto.com / Dave Long, © www.istockphoto.com / David Kahn, © www.istockphoto.com / Alice Scully; © www.istockphoto.com / Leif Norman, © www.istockphoto.com / Ron Bailey; © www.istockphoto.com / jc559; © www.istock-photo.com / Reid Harrington; © www.istockphoto.com / Lora Clark

Designer: Nelson Sá; Editor: Nicholas Croce
Photo Researcher: Marty Levick